Rhode Island

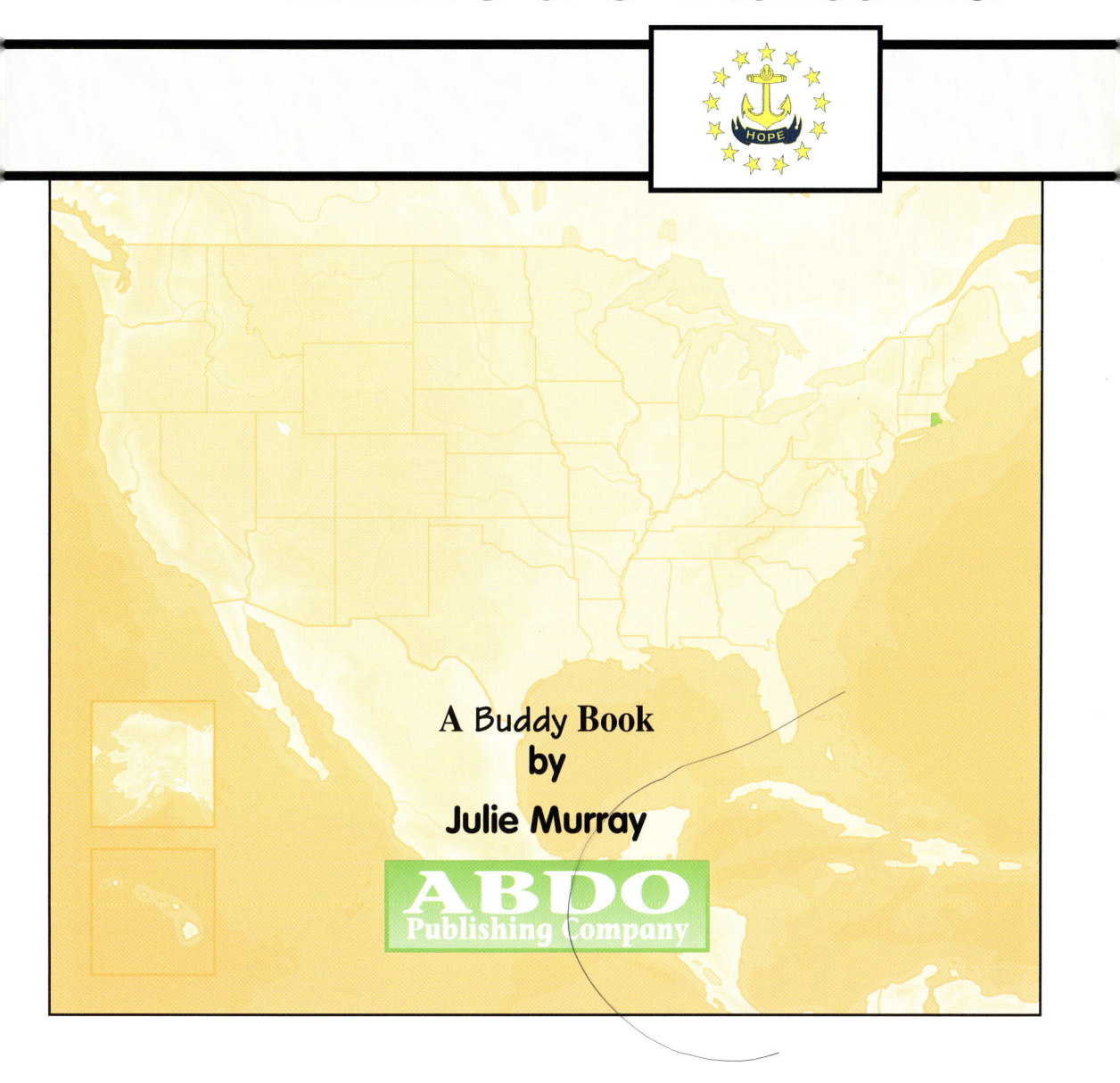

A Buddy Book
by
Julie Murray

ABDO
Publishing Company

VISIT US AT
www.abdopub.com

Published by ABDO Publishing Company, 4940 Viking Drive, Edina, Minnesota 55435.

Copyright © 2006 by Abdo Consulting Group, Inc. International copyrights reserved in all countries. No part of this book may be reproduced in any form without written permission from the publisher. Buddy Books™ is a trademark and logo of ABDO Publishing Company.

Printed in the United States.

Edited by: Sarah Tieck
Contributing Editor: Michael P. Goecke
Graphic Design: Deb Coldiron, Maria Hosley
Image Research: Sarah Tieck
Photographs: AP/Wide World, Clipart.com, Comstock, Fotosearch, Getty Images, Library of Congress, One Mile Up, Photos.com, Scenic Photo, William Johnson

Library of Congress Cataloging-in-Publication Data

Murray, Julie, 1969-
 Rhode Island / Julie Murray.
  p. cm. — (The United States)
 Includes index.
 Contents: A snapshot of Rhode Island — Where is Rhode Island? — All about Rhode Island — Cities and the capital — Famous citizens — Rhode Island's landscape — United States Navy — The Industrial Revolution — A history of Rhode Island.
  ISBN 1-59197-698-7
  1. Rhode Island—Juvenile literature. I. Title.

F79.3.M87 2005
974.5—dc22

2005046219

Table Of Contents

A Snapshot Of Rhode Island 4
Where Is Rhode Island? 8
Fun Facts 12
Cities And The Capital 14
Famous Citizens .16
Rhode Island's Landscape 18
United States Navy 22
The Industrial Revolution 24
A History Of Rhode Island 28
A State Map 30
Important Words .31
Web Sites 31
Index 32

A Snapshot Of Rhode Island

Rhode Island is known as "Little Rhody." That is because of the small size of this state. Rhode Island may be small, but it has a big history. Rhode Island was the first state to allow religious freedom. It was also the birthplace of the **Industrial Revolution**.

Machinery like this came into use during the Industrial Revolution.

Rhode Island's coast borders the Atlantic Ocean.

There are 50 states in the United States. Every state is different. Every state has an official **nickname**. Rhode Island's nickname is "The Ocean State." This is because the state has 384 miles (618 km) of coastline. Only about 40 miles (64 km) of that coastline directly borders the Atlantic Ocean. The rest borders bays, inlets, and islands.

Rhode Island became the 13th state on May 29, 1790. It only has 1,213 square miles (3,142 sq km) of land. It is home to 1,048,319 people.

Where Is Rhode Island?

There are four parts of the United States. Each part is called a region. Each region is in a different area of the country. The United States Census Bureau says the four regions are the Northeast, the South, the Midwest, and the West.

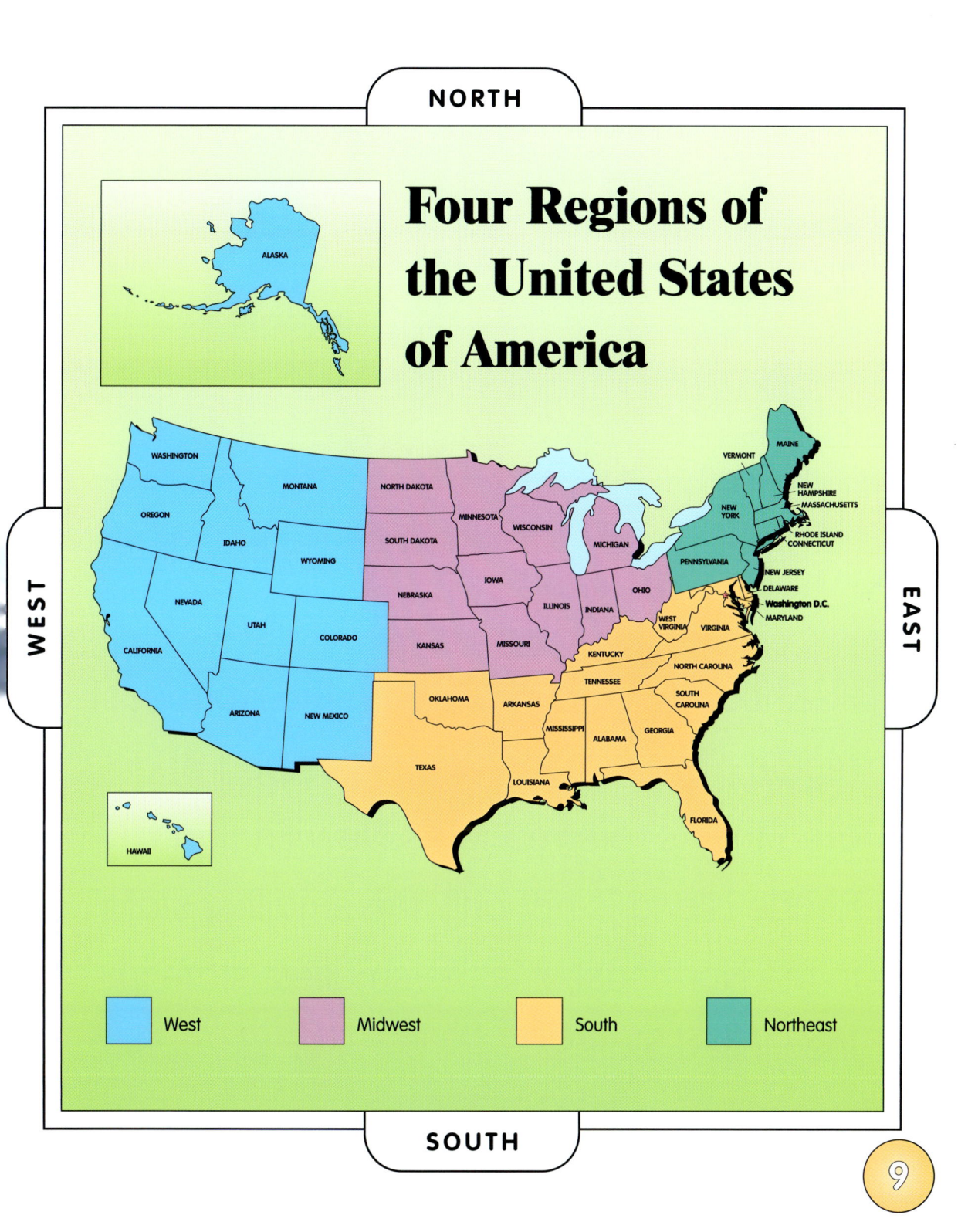

Four Regions of the United States of America

NORTH · SOUTH · EAST · WEST

- West
- Midwest
- South
- Northeast

Many people fish in the waters near Rhode Island.

Rhode Island is located in the Northeast region of the United States. It is part of an area that is referred to as New England. Rhode Island is not only the smallest state in the Northeast, it is the smallest state in the United States.

Rhode Island is bordered by two other states and a body of water. Massachusetts is to the north and east. Connecticut is west. The Atlantic Ocean forms the state's southern border.

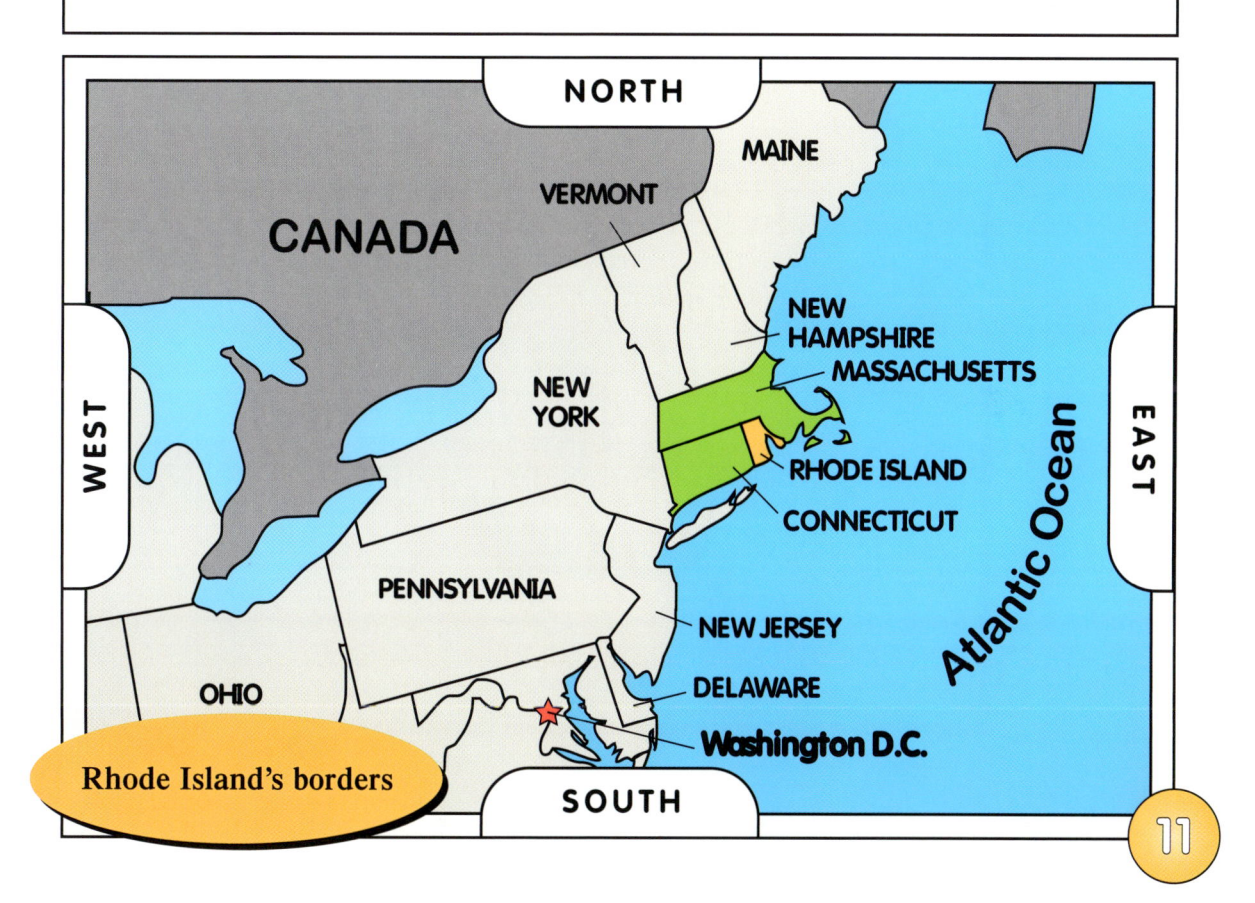

Rhode Island's borders

Fun Facts

Rhode Island

State abbreviation: **RI**
State nickname: The Ocean State
State capital: Providence
State motto: Hope
Statehood: May 29, 1790, 13th state
Population: 1,048,319, ranks 43rd
Land area: 1,213 square miles (3,142 sq km), ranks 50th

State flag: Adopted in 1897

State song: "Rhode Island's It for Me"

State government: Three branches: legislative, executive, and judicial

Average July temperature: 71°F (22°C)

Average January temperature: 29°F (-2°C)

State flower: Violet

State tree: Red maple

State bird: Rhode Island red hen

Cities And The Capital

The Rhode Island Statehouse

Providence is the **capital** of Rhode Island. It is also the largest city in the state. Providence is a seaport. It is part of Narragansett Bay. Providence was the first city in the United States to allow religious freedom. This means people can choose their own religion.

Warwick is the second-largest city in the state. Warwick is also located near the shores of Narragansett Bay. It is part of a metropolitan area that includes Providence, Rhode Island, and Fall River, Massachusetts.

A view of Providence.

Famous Citizens

Roger Williams (1603?–1683)

Roger Williams was born in London, England. He was a clergyman who believed in religious freedom. He established Rhode Island. He did this to create a place where people could choose their own religion. Williams also founded the city of Providence.

A statue of Roger Williams.

Famous Citizens

Gilbert Stuart (1755–1828)

Gilbert Stuart was born in Saunderstown. He was an artist. He is famous for painting a portrait of George Washington. Today, this portrait appears on the United States $1 bill.

Gilbert Stuart

Rhode Island's Landscape

Rhode Island is small. It is 48 miles (77 km) from the northern border to the southern border. It is 37 miles (60 km) from the eastern border to the western border.

Southern and eastern Rhode Island is made up of low-lying land. This area is known as the Coastal Lowlands. There are sandy beaches, rocky cliffs, salt ponds, and lagoons. Narragansett Bay cuts into the state. Many of Rhode Island's major cities are located along Narragansett Bay.

One of Rhode Island's sandy beaches.

Newport Harbor is in Rhode Island.

Rhode Island includes 36 islands. Most of these islands are found in Narragansett Bay. The largest is Aquidneck Island. Block Island is the only island outside of the bay.

Northwestern Rhode Island has forests, hills, lakes, and ponds. Jerimoth Hill is the state's highest point. It stands 812 feet (248 m) high.

A view of northwestern Rhode Island.

United States Navy

The United States Navy has a long history in Rhode Island. In 1775, the Continental Navy was founded in Rhode Island. This was the beginning of the United States Navy.

Today, the United States Navy is still a big part of Rhode Island. The Naval War College is located in Newport. Officers and navy personnel receive advanced training there.

A United States Navy ship.

The Industrial Revolution

The **Industrial Revolution** in the United States started in Rhode Island.

A man named Samuel Slater is known as the "Father of the Industrial Revolution." Slater got his start as a mill manager in England. Back then, people who worked in England's factories weren't allowed to leave the country. This is because they wanted to keep the machines in their mills a secret.

Slater snuck out of England. He pretended to be a farmer and came to the United States. In 1790, he built a cotton mill in Pawtucket that used water power. He used the power of the Blackstone River to run his cotton mill.

One of Samuel Slater's first mills.

An old-fashioned cotton mill.

After Slater's mill was running, more cotton mills were built. People realized that it was faster and cheaper to have machines make the products than to have people do the work by hand. Soon factories were producing tools, machines, and even jewelry. Today, Rhode Island produces a lot of jewelry.

A History Of
Rhode Island

1524: Giovanni da Verrazzano visits Narragansett Bay.

1636: Roger Williams establishes Providence.

1790: Rhode Island becomes the 13th state on May 29.

1917: Rhode Island women win the right to vote in presidential elections.

1954: The first Jazz Festival is held in Newport.

1969: Newport Bridge is completed. This connects the cities of Newport and Jamestown.

1990: Rhode Island celebrates its **bicentennial**.

1991: Hurricane Bob hits Rhode Island.

1996: A large amount of oil spills into Block Island Sound.

2004: Newport hosts the 50th JVC Jazz Festival.

Sometimes, hurricanes cause flooding in New England.

A State Map

Cities In Rhode Island

- Pawtucket
- Providence ★
- Warwick
- Saunderstown
- Jamestown
- Aquidneck Island
- Newport
- Block Island

Important Words

bicentennial 200-year anniversary.

capital a city where government leaders meet.

Industrial Revolution the time from 1780 to 1860 when power-driven machinery was introduced to make goods.

nickname a name that describes something special about a person or a place.

Web Sites

To learn more about Rhode Island, visit ABDO Publishing Company on the World Wide Web. Web site links about Rhode Island are featured on our Book Links page. These links are routinely monitored and updated to provide the most current information available.

www.abdopub.com

Index

Aquidneck Island	**20, 30**
Atlantic Ocean	**6, 7, 11**
Blackstone River	**25**
Block Island	**20, 30**
Block Island Sound	**29**
Connecticut	**11**
Continental Navy	**22**
England	**16, 24, 25**
Fall River, Massachusetts	**15**
Industrial Revolution	**4, 5, 24, 25**
Jamestown	**28, 30**
Jerimoth Hill	**21**
Massachusetts	**11, 15**
Midwest	**8, 9**
Narragansett Bay	**14, 15, 18, 20, 28**
Naval War College	**22**
New England	**10, 29**
Newport	**20, 22, 28, 29, 30**
Northeast	**8, 9, 10**
Pawtucket	**25, 30**
Providence	**12, 14, 15, 16, 28, 30**
Saunderstown	**17, 30**
Slater, Samuel	**24, 25, 27**
South	**8, 9**
Stuart, Gilbert	**17**
United States Census Bureau	**8**
United States Navy	**22, 23**
Verrazzano, Giovanni da	**28**
Warwick	**15, 30**
Washington, George	**17**
West	**8, 9**
Williams, Roger	**16, 28**